TONY EVANS
SPEAKS OUT ON
SPIRITUAL WARFARE

D1468667

TONY EVANS
SPEAKS OUT ON
SPIRITUAL
WARFARE

MOODY PRESS
CHICAGO

ISBN: 0-8024-4369-9

5 7 9 10 8 6

Printed in the United States of America

SPIRITUAL WARFARE

Remember that old newsreel that shows President Franklin Roosevelt addressing Congress the day after the Japanese attack on Pearl Harbor in December of 1941?

Talking about "a day that will live in infamy," the president declared that in reality, America was already at war. Roosevelt just needed a declaration of Congress to make it official.

I am not the president, but I have a declaration to make: You and I are at war! In fact, we are engaged right now in the mother of all battles. No war in history can compare with the battle you and I are fighting. It can be the cause of either your greatest joy as a Christian or your deepest pain.

THE AGENDA IN SPIRITUAL WARFARE

The war I am talking about is the spiritual warfare

that you became a part of the day you received Jesus Christ as your Savior. This war affects every area of your life. There is no way you can avoid the conflict. There is no bunker or foxhole you can crawl into that will shield you from the effects of this cosmic battle between the forces of God and the forces of Satan.

You may not even know you're at war. A lot of Christians don't. But other people can see the results of the battle in those people's lives, because they have become casualties of spiritual warfare.

Some Christians are emotional casualties of spiritual warfare. They are discouraged, depressed, downtrodden, and defeated. Others are marital and family casualties. Divorce, conflict, and abuse are some of the "battle scars" these believers bear.

Still others have been wounded morally in the battle. They cannot control their passions, or they make poor moral choices. For some Christians, the wounds have been inflicted on their finances. They are losing the financial battle because they are losing the spiritual battle. It's not just a matter of how they use their credit cards.

Since we are all at war, and since there is so much at stake both here on earth and in eternity, we'd better find out what spiritual warfare is all about and how to fight the battle successfully. That's what I want to help you do in this book.

The Essence of the Battle

Let me begin by stating the obvious. The essence of

our warfare is spiritual. Because of this, the degree to which we will be successful is the degree to which we are prepared to understand and fight this battle on a spiritual level.

Perhaps a definition will help at this point. Spiritual warfare is that conflict being waged in the invisible, spiritual realm that is being manifest in the visible, physical realm.

In other words, spiritual warfare is a battle between invisible, angelic forces that affects you and me. The cause of the war is something you and I can't see. But the effects are very visible in the kinds of problems I mentioned above, and in the day-to-day stuff you and I face all the time.

It's hard enough to fight an enemy you can see. It's much harder to fight someone you can't see. That is exactly the kind of enemy we face. Paul wrote, "Our struggle is not against flesh and blood, but against the rulers, against the powers, against the world forces of this darkness, against the spiritual forces of wickedness in the heavenly places" (Ephesians 6:12).

This verse identifies the enemy: Satan and his demons. That means we are making a grand mistake if we think people are the real enemy. People can be bad, no doubt. But they are merely conduits for this greater battle. Satan has been very successful in getting us to fight people, rather than fighting that which is causing people to be the way they are.

Let me set down a foundational principle for spiritual warfare. Everything we see in the physical realm is either caused, influenced, or provoked by something in the spiritual realm. Your five senses are not the limit of reality.

Daniel 4:32 states that heaven rules over all the affairs of earth. So until we address the spiritual cause of a problem, we will never fix the physical effect of that problem.

Not only are our physical senses very limited, but they are often of little help in spiritual warfare. If we are going to wage successful spiritual battle, we need a "sixth sense"—a keen awareness of the spiritual realm. In order to understand spiritual warfare, we have to address it through the lens of the spirit, with the help of the Holy Spirit.

The Impact of the Battle

Even though this battle is spiritual, it has very definite effects in the physical realm. You know you're in a battle when you get shot and start bleeding. We are seeing the "bleeding," the impact, of spiritual warfare in at least four areas of life today.

Many believers are seeing the wounds of spiritual warfare in their personal lives. This doesn't mean these people are necessarily doing something really bad. It could be that they have a problem such as uncontrolled anger.

Our emotions can give the devil an entry into our lives. Paul explained the relationship between our emotions and spiritual warfare: "Therefore, laying aside falsehood, speak truth each one of you with his neighbor, for we are members of one another. Be angry, and yet do not sin; do not let the sun go down on your anger, and do not give the devil an opportunity" (Ephesians 4:25–27).

Failing to control anger grants the devil an opportunity to get a foothold in your life. Then he can use it as a base of operation to launch more spiritual attacks against you.

Many Christians are suffering today because of anger that was not resolved yesterday—and anger is just one of a complex range of human emotions. If Satan can seize our emotions, he can destroy our ability to function by crippling us emotionally or leading us into all manner of destructive and addictive behavior.

Many believers are also feeling the effects of spiritual warfare in their families. The devil messed up the first family in the Garden of Eden, and we have been dealing with the effects of that sin ever since.

Here's a specific example of family relationships and spiritual warfare. Paul wrote to husbands and wives in 1 Corinthians 7:5, "Stop depriving one another, except by agreement for a time, so that you may devote yourselves to prayer, and come together again so that Satan will not tempt you because of your lack of self-control."

Paul is saying that when a husband and wife don't have a fulfilling sexual relationship, the devil sees that lack as an opportunity to come in and bring about moral destruction in the family. So this thing of spiritual warfare gets right down to the nitty-gritty aspects of everyday life.

The Location of the Battle

Where in the universe is this great battle called spiritual warfare being fought? Paul tells us it is "in the heavenly places" (Ephesians 6:12).

The third heaven is the throne room of God, the place we normally think of when we hear the word *heaven*. The Bible has the most to say about this heaven. In fact, heaven is a very busy place, the sphere of God's operation.

In the book of Ephesians alone, we find numerous references to heavenly places in addition to the one above. I want to review these with you, because understanding how to tap into the heavenly places is crucial to spiritual warfare.

Ephesians 1:3 says, "Blessed be the God and Father of our Lord Jesus Christ, who has blessed us with every spiritual blessing in the heavenly places in Christ." God resides in the heavenly places, and so do *all* of our spiritual blessings.

This is important because if you are engaged in a spiritual battle and need help to win, the help you need is with God the Father, who is in the heavenly places. But if you don't know how to get to heavenly places, you won't know how to get to the heavenly help you need to win the battle in earthly places.

According to Ephesians 1:20, when God the Father raised Jesus Christ from the dead, He seated His Son "at His right hand in the heavenly places." Not only are the Father and your blessings in heavenly places, Jesus

Christ is there too. So if you need Christ's help in earthly places, you'd better know where He is hanging out and how to take a trip there to obtain His help in your warfare.

But it gets even better. God also "raised us up with [Christ], and seated us with Him in the heavenly places" (Ephesians 2:6). Do you get the picture here? You and I as believers are also in heavenly places.

You may say, "Wait a minute, I'm here on earth. I'm in a physical place." But that's a problem. If you only see where you are physically and never understand where you're supposed to be spiritually, you'll never be able to win in spiritual warfare.

Satan is a limited being.

Paul is saying that when you accepted Christ, you were transported to another sphere. Even though your body is limited to earth, your spirit that should be controlling your body is operating in a wholly different realm.

What else is in heavenly places? Spiritual rulers and authorities (see Ephesians 3:10). These are angels. This is important for spiritual warfare, because it takes an angel to beat an angel. Remember, Satan and his demons are also "in the heavenly places" (6:12).

See, if your problem originates in the heavenly places, you need a solution that originates in the heavenly places. Most of us have very little consciousness of angels because they're not part of our physical world. But we need to understand that the angels of God and the demons of hell are the "foot soldiers" in the cosmic battle between God and Satan.

When you hear believers say they are being attacked by the devil, they probably mean they are being harassed by his foot soldiers. Satan is a limited being. He is not everywhere present, all-knowing, and all-powerful like God.

But Satan does have a whole host of evil angels called demons he can use for spiritual attacks. So anything that hell can bring against you is the result of satanic activity in the same realm in which God operates, called heavenly places.

You and I are no match for the power and deceptiveness of Satan and his army. We need the power of God to neutralize and destroy the power of Satan.

But if you need divine help and don't yet have a "heavenly places" mind-set, you won't know how to get the help you need at the time you need it. Since everything related to our warfare is in the spiritual realm, we need to know how to reach into the heavenly places for help. That's where the action is.

The good news is, you can take a trip to heaven any time you feel like it—because spiritually, you're already there. You are seated with Christ in heavenly places.

Some years ago, my wife Lois and I were in London, England, staying at a hotel that was one block from the American embassy. Embassies are sovereign territories, belonging to the country they represent.

The American embassy is a little piece of America on foreign soil. So if you are an American citizen in a foreign country and you need help or protection, you go to the American embassy.

That's what "heavenly places" means. It's the embassy of heaven on foreign soil. It's the place where you can make contact with your homeland.

The Bible says that we are aliens on earth, just passing through on our way to heaven. God wants us to use our visa while we are here, but live like people who belong to another realm.

We can be thankful that God has established His "embassy" in heavenly places, because there's a war on out there. The kingdom of darkness has its own king, Satan, and he wants to be in charge of the universe.

However, there is no question that the kingdom of God and His King, Jesus Christ, are firmly in charge. Jesus' eternal victory is already assured. But God has allowed us to choose in our individual lives who will be in charge.

Those of us who have decided for Christ will live eternally with Him. But while we're here on earth, we still need to decide for Christ each day in terms of our spiritual warfare.

The Forces in the Battle

As I said before, this is angelic conflict. The archangel Michael and the holy angels are fighting Satan and the angels who rebelled with him, as described in Revelation 12:7–12.

This war in heaven directly affects what is happening on earth. We are in the midst of an angelic conflict, a satanic rebellion, in which Satan is seeking to bring this whole world under his domain. That means when you were born into the kingdom of God, you were born into a war.

We are surrounded by our spiritual enemy, but the battle is not for land or anything physical. This cosmic battle is for *glory*. The issue is, Who is going to get the glory in this universe? Who is going to be worshiped?

Satan has said to God, "You cannot have all the glory in creation. I want the glory for myself."

God's response was, "My glory I will not give to another" (Isaiah 48:11).

Satan said, "You are going to share Your glory with me. Let's go to war." The battle is for the throne of creation. Praise God the outcome has never been in doubt, but the battle goes on every day in our lives as to who will get the glory by what we do.

That's why Paul told us, "Whatever you do, do all to the glory of God" (1 Corinthians 10:31; see also Colossians 3:23). This is the essence of the battle.

I don't know where you are in your Christian life, so I don't know where you stand in relation to the reality of spiritual warfare. You may not realize the Christian life is a war. Or you may know there's a war on, and you have the battle scars to prove it. You may have been tasting defeat at the hands of Satan.

Paul said in Colossians 1:13 that everyone who comes to Jesus Christ for salvation is delivered from the domain of the devil. When you received Jesus as your Savior and Lord, God set you free.

You may be wondering, "If God set me free, why am I still in bondage to the devil in my daily life? If I'm on the winning side, why am I losing so often?"

There can be a number of answers to that question, but many believers are suffering defeat in spiritual warfare because they are trying to fight Satan in their own strength.

I have news for you. Satan isn't afraid of you at all! He's not afraid of me either. But he cannot stand up against God for even a second.

This is why Paul wrote, "Be strong in the Lord and in the strength of His might. Put on the full armor of God, so that you will be able to stand firm against the schemes of the devil" (Ephesians 6:10–11). It is when God fights the battle for you, not when *you* fight the battle for you, that you win against the Evil One.

Lack of victory in the spiritual battle reflects a lack of understanding of our divine resources. Every Christian has problems, but it's the inability to move beyond the problem, the inability to get past the failure, that keeps us in spiritual defeat. Victory is found in dependence on God, so Satan's plan is to detach us from dependence on God.

Since we're talking about our enemy in this cosmic struggle called spiritual warfare, let's look at Satan and his strategy in more detail so we'll know who and what we're up against.

THE ADVERSARY IN SPIRITUAL WARFARE

The story is told of a farmer who was constantly having his watermelons stolen by thieves.

So the farmer came up with a brilliant idea to thwart the thieves. He poisoned one watermelon, then put a sign in his watermelon field that read: "Warning: one of these watermelons has been poisoned."

The next day the farmer went out to find that none of his melons had been stolen, because the thieves didn't know which one was poisoned. He was quite satisfied that his idea had worked and that he would not have a problem with theft anymore.

But the day after that, the farmer came out to his field to find that someone had scratched through his sign and had changed the wording to say, "Two of these watermelons have been poisoned." The farmer had to destroy his whole crop because now he didn't know which other melon was poisoned.

That's what it is like to deal with the devil. No matter what you come up with, he can come up with something better. No matter what sign you put up, he can change the wording. No matter what strategy you devise, you can't outwit this fellow.

Satan has a definite strategy, and it can be understood in one word: deception. Satan's strategy for your life and mine is to deceive us. He is the master deceiver. He is the camouflage king.

The reason Satan has turned to deception is that he cannot "outpower" God. Satan tried to overcome God in heaven, and that gamble failed. Satan's power will never be a match for God's.

Evidently, in his rebellion Satan forgot that God can do something he cannot do, which is create something out of nothing by simply speaking it into existence.

Satan cannot create anything. All he can do is manipulate and maneuver what has been created. Since he cannot match God's power, Satan has to maximize the power he has, and deception is his strong suit. He has turned deception into an art form.

The Power of Satan's Strategy

That Satan is no match for God doesn't mean he is powerless. In fact, I want to begin the discussion of Satan's strategy by looking at the power of his deception.

In 2 Thessalonians 2, Paul was correcting these believers' misconceptions about the Day of the Lord:

> Let no one in any way deceive you, for it will not come unless the apostasy comes first, and the man of lawlessness is revealed, the son of destruction, who opposes and exalts himself above every so-called god or object of worship, so that he takes his seat in the temple of God, displaying himself as being God. (vv. 3–4)

Paul then said that this "lawless one," the Antichrist, will not appear until God's restraint is removed. Then, "that lawless one will be revealed . . . the one whose coming is in accord with the activity of Satan, with all power and signs and false wonders, and with all the deception of wickedness for those who perish" (vv. 8–10).

The appearance of the Antichrist will be Satan's crowning achievement in his plan to deceive the world. The Antichrist will be empowered by Satan, who will give this person great power to pull off the master deception—masquerading as God.

But we don't have to wait until the end times to see the power of Satan at work. How else can you explain the fact that people will give up everything they have to move in with a cult and put themselves under someone else's power, even to the point of committing suicide in the name of God? The only explanation is Satan's deception.

Where does Satan get the power he wields over people? He gets it from what I call his constitutional superiority over any man or woman. By this I mean that Satan is an angel, a spirit being. He does not have the limitations of flesh and blood.

Therefore, you and I can't compete with the devil in our own strength. We can't outsmart the master deceiver. He has authority by virtue of his person. Satan's authority is given by God and limited by God, but it is still a greater authority than you and I exercise.

Satan is also powerful by virtue of his vast experience. He has untold years of experience at being the devil. You are not the first human being he has come up against. He has been against smarter and stronger people than you and me, and he has won.

One thing Satan has learned during all these years is how to make himself look like one of the good guys (see 2 Corinthians 11:14). He is the master chameleon. He can become any color he needs to be in order to camouflage himself and his plans.

Satan is so experienced at deception that the Bible says one day he will deceive all the nations of the world (Revelation 20:8). This world is a puppet, and Satan holds the strings.

Another reason that Satan is so powerful in carrying out his strategy is that he commands a massive organization of evil (Ephesians 6:12). Satan's organization is well run and heavily disguised.

It reminds me of the Mafia. Do you know the address of Mafia headquarters? Can you pick out members of the Mafia as they walk the streets? The Mafia has camouflaged itself. Its members operate legitimate-looking businesses behind which they hide their crimes. We know that they are out there and that they are powerful, but they're hard to identify.

Satan heads a spiritual Mafia that controls people and even nations. People wonder how a nation can produce a Stalin or a Hitler. The explanation is the massive work and deception of Satan. That's how powerful he is.

The Program of Satan's Strategy

Let's consider Satan's program. What is he hoping to achieve by his strategy of deception?

Satan's program is to produce such a wonderful

counterfeit of God's works and ways that he leads us astray. Paul wrote to the Corinthians, "I am afraid that, as the serpent deceived Eve by his craftiness, your minds will be led astray from the simplicity and purity of devotion to Christ" (2 Corinthians 11:3).

Notice that Paul's illustration of Satan's deception is Eve, which takes us back to Genesis 3. Satan hasn't changed his program since the Garden of Eden when he led Eve astray.

Satan is a counterfeiter—and the better the counterfeiter, the fewer the number of people who realize they're carrying counterfeit money. In fact, you can buy groceries and gas and furniture with counterfeit money. The problem is when those bills hit the bank and are shown to be worthless.

You'll remember that Satan told Eve she could be like God. He knew that was a counterfeit promise because he had tried that himself. But he's still out there tempting us to take things into our own hands, to set up our own kingdoms, to try to live independently of God. The devil wants you to believe that you don't have to answer to God anymore.

But that's a myth. This universe is God's house, and He's just letting us live in a borrowed room for a while. At one time or another, most parents have to have an "ownership" discussion with their teenagers. It works like this. A teenager is being rebellious or whatever, so he gets mad, goes to his room, and cranks up the music because he doesn't want to hear what you're saying. So you confront his rebellion and tell him to turn the music down. He responds, "I can do whatever I want in here. This is *my* room."

Wrong. This is where you bring out your homeowner papers and inform your child that since you are paying for the house it belongs to you, not to him. He is simply occupying a room that you let him sleep in.

If he wants his own room, he needs to buy his own house and furniture. Then he can have any room he wants. But until then, it's your room on loan to him, and you as the parent call the shots.

There's a big difference between being the owner of the house and a guest in the house. To me, one of the absolutely foundational verses in Scripture is Psalm 24:1: "The earth is the Lord's, and all it contains, the world, and those who dwell in it."

Everything you and I have belongs to God. And the moment we say, "It's mine," in the sense of ownership as opposed to stewardship, what we've done is insult God by saying, "I want to be like the Most High."

Satan also told Eve, "If you eat of this tree, you will know good and evil." In other words, you can make your own decisions about what's right and wrong. You don't need God's ideas of morality.

Satan also told Eve, "You won't die if you eat from this tree. God was lying to you." In other words, there are no consequences to your actions. You can do whatever you want without suffering any penalties. God won't do anything about it.

But the death God warned Adam and Eve about did come to pass. They lost their innocence, their relationship with Him, and their home in the garden. And physical death followed as the inevitable consequence of their spiritual death.

Whatever label you give to Satan's deception, the basis is the same. Satan hates truth, and he'll try to lead people astray from it every time.

He even has his own fake form of Christianity. He has phony doctrine (1 Timothy 4:1), can produce phony miracles, and has a counterfeit communion table. "You cannot drink the cup of the Lord and the cup of demons" (1 Corinthians 10:21). He also has a fake gospel and spirituality (Galatians 1:11; 3:2–3).

And to propagate his program, the devil has his own false teachers. Paul warned the church at Corinth of men who were "false apostles, deceitful workers, disguising themselves as apostles of Christ" (2 Corinthians 11:13).

The Process of Satan's Strategy

We've seen that Satan's strategy is powerful and purposeful. Now we need to talk about the process of his deception, how it actually works.

The apostle James outlined the process by which Satan deceives people. It begins with the desire: "Let no one say when he is tempted, 'I am being tempted by God'; for God cannot be tempted by evil, and He Himself does not tempt anyone. But each one is tempted when he is carried away and enticed by his own lust" (James 1:13–14).

Stage one in Satan's plan is the arousal of a desire.

We have many legitimate desires. But these desires become a problem when Satan tempts us to meet a legitimate desire in an illegitimate way.

Satan knows you can't just skip the desire, because desires are God-given. So the enemy wants to control how your desires are met. This is the issue in temptation. Satan wants your desires to master you, rather than you mastering your desires.

In stage two of the process, the sinful growth of a desire leads to deception, the moment the person takes Satan's bait and finds out he has been deceived.

Satan is a smart fisherman. He's not just throwing bare hooks out in front of us. He doesn't say to a man, "Come on down to the local bar and let me get you addicted to alcohol so you can lose your job and your family, lose your self-respect and self-control, and wind up in a rehab center."

Satan is far too smart to let his hooks show. He covers them with enticing bait. Satan deceives us by planting the evil thought or idea in our minds. He can't make us do anything, but he can build deceitful castles of desire in our minds.

Desire leads to deception, and then deception leads to disobedience, which is stage three of the process. "When lust has conceived, it gives birth to sin" (James 1:15).

James used the analogy of conception, pregnancy, and birth because the birth process so closely parallels the temptation process. When a temptation is welcomed and acted upon, that act of conception produces a "child" called sin. And once a child has been conceived, its birth is sure to follow.

In other words, committing disobedience is like the act of procreation. The result always shows up after a while. And like any other child, sin will begin to grow once it has been born.

Let me tell you why sin is a child you don't want to have. Children operate by their feelings. All children know is, "I want this. I want that. Give me this. Give me that." Sin will keep you living by your feelings, and when you live by feelings you do things based on how they make you feel, not whether they are right or wrong.

Don't ever think you have it better with Satan than you do with God.

God wants us to live like mature adults, people who make decisions based on their will, not their feelings. You may not feel like getting up and going to work every morning, but you get up and go anyway because it's your responsibility and you are acting on your will. Your maturity overrides your feelings of the moment.

Part of becoming mature in Christ is learning to submit our feelings to our will, to operate on the basis of what we know to be true rather than just what we feel. But sin will keep us spiritually immature, a slave to our emotions.

The fourth and final stage in Satan's process is death. James said, "When sin is accomplished, it brings forth death" (James 1:15).

Sin certainly brings spiritual death. That is one of the fundamental truths we learn from the sin of Adam and Eve. Sin can also produce physical death in some cases.

Satan brings death and destruction with him, but God is the source of "every perfect gift" (James 1:17). So James said, "Do not be deceived, my beloved brethren" (v. 16). When Satan deceives and leads us into sin, he causes us to miss the goodness of God. Don't ever think you have it better with Satan than you do with God. Satan's road leads to death if we follow it.

The Purpose of Satan's Strategy

Now that we know the process Satan wants to take us through, we are ready to talk about the purpose behind his strategy. Satan has several major purposes behind his deceptions.

For believers, one of Satan's purposes is to interrupt the process by which God gets glory through our lives. He wants to render us ineffective in terms of any real impact for Christ.

That's why he keeps some believers depressed, some discouraged, and others underneath their circumstances. He wants you there because he knows

nothing for God if you're miserable. God
glory if you're too miserable to give it to Him.
In fact, Satan can twist things so much that he'll get you blaming God for your misery. And if you're not careful, the devil can wind up using you to bring un-happiness and misery to others.

The devil also wants to deflect you and me from do-ing the will of God by frustrating God's will for our lives. Satan even tried to frustrate the accomplishment of God's will in Jesus' life. Satan didn't know God's will for His Son was the cross, but in the wilderness the devil tempted Jesus to take the easy way.

Satan also used one of Jesus' own disciples to try to turn Him away from following His Father's will (Matthew 16:21–22). Imagine Peter rebuking Jesus, try-ing to tell Him where He was wrong. Only Satan could have thought of an attack this bold. Jesus knew who was behind it, because He told Peter, "Get behind Me, Satan!" (v. 23). The devil didn't understand why Jesus came to earth, but he was trying to frustrate God's plan. Peter was agreeing with the devil's plan. He was thinking and speaking out of two sides of his mind. He was a double-minded man.

Jesus was saying, "Get behind Me, devil. I have to go to the cross. Peter, Satan is using you, one of My children, to stop Me from doing My Father's will."

If Satan wasn't afraid to try and turn Jesus away from God's will, do you think he will leave us alone? Of course not.

As a matter of fact, Jesus went on to say in this

same passage, "If anyone wishes to come after Me, he must deny himself, and take up his cross and follow Me" (Matthew 16:24). Satan tried to get Jesus to focus on the suffering of the cross instead of the glory of the resurrection. Our enemy will do the same to us.

Let's face it. The cross does involve suffering. It's an instrument of death. Bearing my cross means I am willing to identify publicly with Jesus Christ and accept anything that goes with that identification. It means I will bear the scars of being identified with Christ. But the cross is also the path to resurrection glory.

The Historical Defeat of Satan

Satan is powerful and purposeful and deceptive, but he's also a defeated foe. I want to close this section of our study on spiritual warfare by talking about Satan's historical defeat at the cross and his eternal defeat at the end of time.

Looking ahead to the cross, Jesus said, "Now judgment is upon this world; now the ruler of this world will be cast out. And I, if I am lifted up from the earth, will draw all men to Myself" (John 12:31–32). The cross was the ultimate defeat that Satan did not anticipate.

When Jesus Christ was on earth, He let the devil know there was one Man he couldn't mess with. Jesus tied up the "strong man," the devil, so He could plunder the devil's house (Matthew 12:29). Jesus had total control over Satan's demons. They had to do what He said, because He was and is infinitely stronger than the devil.

But it was in His death that Jesus really crushed the head of Satan. Satan was judged at the cross (John 12:31; 16:7–11), because on the cross God removed the curse of sin that Satan caused to be laid on mankind in the Garden of Eden.

Satan was banking on a fact that he knew about God because he had experienced it himself. The fact is this: When you sin, you come under God's curse. There is nowhere to run from it. The Bible says that anyone who does not keep God's law perfectly is under a curse (Galatians 3:10).

Sin is the failure to keep God's law. It is a falling short of His perfect standard. The reason people will spend eternity in hell is that when they sin, they fall under the curse of God's broken law. If that failure is not addressed in Christ, eternal judgment must follow.

But Jesus removed the curse of sin, which was the curse of the law (Galatians 3:13). Law becomes a curse when Satan uses it to trip us up. You see, if he can't lead us into a life of sin, he will tempt us to go the other direction, that of trying to please God by our goodness. Satan doesn't care how we arrive in hell, just so we get there.

Satan has a lot of people believing they are good enough to keep God's law and earn their way into heaven. But since no one except Christ has ever kept God's law, all those who try to follow it break it and come under His curse. Satan loves to put people under the same curse he is under. But on the cross Jesus lifted the curse. The Cross turned what was our judgment into our blessing.

The Eternal Defeat of Satan

Satan was not only defeated in history at the cross. He will be defeated in the future, which is already as good as done from God's viewpoint.

When Satan's eternal sentence is executed, our enemy will be put away forever. He will be banished to hell for eternity as God carries out the final stage of Satan's judgment.

In Revelation 12:7–12 we see the final war in which Satan will be "thrown down" (v. 9). No wonder this elicits great rejoicing on the part of God's saints. Finally, Satan will no longer have even temporary access to heaven.

The last we hear of Satan is in Revelation 20:7–10, which describes the devil's confinement during the millennial reign of Christ, his last gasp of rebellion, and his eternal judgment.

At the end of the Millennium, those who didn't want Jesus to rule over them will get a final opportunity to rebel. Satan will be released to bring out the rebellion that they harbored in their hearts for the thousand years in which Christ reigned.

But the battle will be over quickly, because fire will come down from God and devour them (v. 9). And then will come the moment that God's people have been waiting for: "The devil who deceived them was thrown into the lake of fire and brimstone, where the beast and the false prophet are also; and they will be tormented day and night forever and ever" (v. 10).

Satan's judgment was pronounced in heaven in eternity past, and in Revelation 20 we hear the "thunderclap" that follows the lightning as he is thrown into the lake of fire. There is no question about Satan's final defeat and eternal destiny. He was beaten the moment he rebelled against God in heaven.

OUR AUTHORITY IN SPIRITUAL WARFARE

Now that we know something about the agenda of the battle and the adversary we're up against, I want to show you the authority we have in Christ to wage spiritual warfare.

To do that, we are going to unfold Ephesians 6:10–17, one of *the* foundational passages on spiritual warfare in God's Word. Let's talk about the nature of the armor, the need for the armor, and the names of the armor.

The Nature of Our Armor

The apostle Paul doesn't waste any time in spelling out the nature of the authority we have for spiritual warfare. It's "the full armor of God" (Ephesians 6:11).

But before Paul gets to the armor, he gives us an important exhortation: "Be strong in the Lord and in the strength of His might" (v. 10).

This says the battle is the Lord's, not ours. It is a passive command. That means God supplies the strength, not us. Our job is to "dress for success" by putting on the armor God supplies.

Six pieces of spiritual armor are named in Ephesians 6, and they are divided into two kinds by the use of two verbs. For the first three pieces of armor, Paul used the verb translated "having" along with another word (see vv. 14–15). But we are told to "take" the final three pieces of armor (vv. 16–17).

The difference is that the first three pieces of armor are things we have already put on. The idea is that we are to wear these pieces all the time, the way we put on our clothes every morning. But the other armor pieces, like the sword and the shield, we pick up as we need them, like a baseball player who picks up his bat when it's his turn to bat.

I want you to see this distinction because it helps us understand how to use the armor God has given us.

The Need for Our Armor

The reason you and I need God's armor is that we are fighting a spiritual enemy (Ephesians 6:12). Let's talk about our need for the armor of God as Paul explained it here. He wrote, "Put on the full armor of God, so that you will be able to stand firm against the schemes of the devil" (v. 11).

The key phrase here is "stand firm," which Paul repeated in verses 13 and 14. We need to put on our armor because of our enemy, because of Christ's victory, and because of the coming "evil day" (v. 13).

We have already talked in detail about the enemy. So let's move to the second reason we need God's armor. This is because of the nature of the victory Christ has won for us. Let me explain.

As we said earlier, Paul told us three times that our goal is to stand firm. That means to hold the ground Jesus has already won for us. Despite what you may have heard from some television preachers, the Bible doesn't tell us to attack Satan. It tells us to stand firm against him.

Why? Because Jesus has already invaded Satan's domain and won back all the territory Adam lost. So our job is to hold the ground Jesus has won, not to fight to win. We are fighting *from* a position of victory, not *for* victory.

Ephesians 1:3 says God has already blessed us with every spiritual blessing it was possible to give us. Everything God is ever going to do for you in terms of giving you His power and authority and victory, He has already done. Your spiritual victory has already been won. Your weapons are weapons of authority because of the decisive victory Jesus has won.

A third reason we need our armor is because of "the evil day" (Ephesians 6:13). One translation calls it the time "when things are at their worst" (NEB). It's the time when all hell breaks loose and comes against you.

Are you having it pretty easy right now? Enjoy it, because an evil day is coming. That's not pessimism, just reality.

In 1 Corinthians 16:13 Paul wrote, "Stand firm in the faith." That's the key. We can stand firm if our faith is in the One who provides us with the armor. God wants us to hold our ground and not budge when the evil day comes.

The Names of the Armor

Let's take a brief look at each piece of the armor God has provided for us. These are weapons you must know how to wear and wield to make the most of your spiritual authority in Christ.

The first piece of armor Paul named is the belt of truth. "Stand firm therefore, having girded your loins with truth" (Ephesians 6:14a).

Our spiritual armor is patterned after the armor and weapons of a Roman soldier of the day. For instance, these soldiers wore a long tunic that flowed down to the ground. But when it came time to fight, the soldier would pick up his tunic and tuck it into his belt for mobility in battle.

A Roman soldier also carried his sword on his belt, and his breastplate connected to the belt too. The belt was fundamental, because everything else connected to it. It held everything together.

That's what the truth is designed to do for us spiritually. The truth is an objective standard of reality that stands outside of our experience and stands above our opinions. That standard of truth is the Word of God. It is the beginning point of authority.

The second piece of armor is also found in Ephesians 6:14. "Stand firm therefore . . . having put on the breastplate of righteousness."

The Roman soldier's breastplate protected his heart. What is the best protection for your heart in spiritual warfare? To be covered in Christ's righteousness, reflected in a righteous lifestyle. Righteous living wipes out the conditions in which demons can fester.

This is talking about our salvation. If you know Jesus Christ as your Savior, not only were your sins forgiven; Christ gave you His perfect righteousness. That is, God credited the righteousness of Christ to your spiritual account. You are righteous today, and can live righteously, because of this transfer.

So you don't have to get up in the morning determined to try to be righteous. Instead, you get up in the morning and say, "Because of Christ, I am righteous today." The breastplate of righteousness is part of the armor you wear all the time, because every day you are dressed in Christ's righteousness.

The third piece of our spiritual armor, and the last of the three pieces we wear every day, is the pair of shoes of "the gospel of peace" (Ephesians 6:15). If you are going to stand firm, you definitely need reliable footwear.

Earlier in Ephesians, Paul had said that Jesus is our peace (Ephesians 2:14). So we're still talking about getting dressed up in Jesus. The "gospel of peace," the good news of Jesus Christ, not only brings us truth and righteousness, but it also brings us the peace of God because we have peace with God. As we take steps in life, the good news of our relationship with God will confirm our steps with rest in the soul.

Now we come to the three pieces of the Christian's armor that Paul tells us to take up as the need arises. The first is the shield of faith, which allows us to "extinguish all the flaming arrows of the evil one" (Ephesians 6:16b).

The shield that a Roman soldier carried into battle was about four-and-a-half feet square. It even helped protect the soldier fighting beside the shield-holder. So Roman soldiers lined up side by side in close formation with their shields together, and all of them were covered as they advanced.

The shield of faith that protects us from anything Satan could fire at us is acting on the truth that we say we believe. We take up the shield of faith when we take the truth that we "amened" on Sunday and live it out on Monday.

Satan wants to hit us with as many flaming arrows as he can. That way, while we're fighting one fire he can hit us with another.

How can we put out Satan's fires? Answer: We can't. But the shield of faith can. So if we will act on God's Word and believe Him, God will send His angelic host to snuff out Satan's fiery arrows as they come in. When we operate on the truth we do know, God will take care of what we don't know.

The helmet of salvation (Ephesians 6:17a) is the next piece of armor that gives us authority over the Enemy.

The helmet protects the head, the control center of the body. The purpose of a soldier's helmet was to absorb blows without causing damage to the head, much like a football player's helmet absorbs the shock of blows to his head.

We're talking about the battles you and I face every day. With the helmet of salvation protecting us, we have the authority to get on top of our circumstances, instead of letting our circumstances bury us.

Paul was talking about the use of the Word, not just its existence.

The helmet allows us to say to Satan, "Go ahead and hit me with your best shot, because 'I can do all things through Him who strengthens me'" (see Philippians 4:13). The helmet's visor allows us to see Jesus (Hebrews 2:9) and focus on Him, so we will relate every area of life to our new identity in Christ. But when we develop spiritual Alzheimer's disease, forgetting our identity in Christ, we lose our spiritual authority.

Now we're ready to complete the armor. We do that when we take up "the sword of the Spirit, which is the word of God" (Ephesians 6:17b). This was not the soldier's long sword, but a short, daggerlike sword about ten inches long. It had a needlelike point and was sharp on both sides. It was used for close-in fighting and could do some serious damage.

What's interesting is that the term Paul used for *word* here does not refer to the Bible as a written book of truth, the way we normally think of the Word of God.

Instead, this is *rhema,* the utterance of God, the Word as it is spoken. Paul was talking about the *use* of the Word, not just its existence.

The best example of wielding the Word was the temptation of Jesus. Satan attacked, but Jesus answered, "It is written," and then defeated Satan with the Word. Jesus hit the enemy with the Word, and the battle was over. It's a waste of time to memorize Scripture if we aren't using it in spiritual warfare.

The Access to Authority

Our weapons of spiritual warfare are powerful and complete, but they won't do us a lot of good if we don't know how to use them. Thankfully, the apostle Paul kept on writing, because in the very next verse he gave us the secret to using this great authority from God.

In other words, after describing the Christian's battle dress, Paul told us *how to get dressed,* how to use the authority we possess: "With all prayer and petition pray at all times in the Spirit, and with this in view, be on the alert with all perseverance and petition for all the saints" (Ephesians 6:18).

It is prayer that gains us access to the authority needed for victorious warfare. Prayer is the way we get dressed for battle, so let's talk about the place of prayer in spiritual warfare.

THE SIGNIFICANCE OF PRAYER
IN SPIRITUAL WARFARE

Remember the story of the emperor who had no

clothes? That's the way a lot of us go around spiritually. We're basically naked, unclothed, because prayer is not a dynamic, vital, potent, consistent, controlling, and all-encompassing reality in our Christian lives.

And because we don't have our spiritual clothes on, we wind up being spiritually embarrassed. And worse than that, we are getting mopped up by Satan although God has given us everything we need to defeat our enemy.

One of the first things a commander tries to do in warfare is to establish superiority in the air. The reason is that whoever controls the air war usually controls the war.

One of our problems is that the church is suffering a lot of casualties on the ground because we haven't established superiority in the air—in the heavenly places where the real warfare is taking place and where Jesus Christ has already won the war and established air superiority for all eternity.

The significance of prayer to spiritual warfare is evident in the first word of Ephesians 6:18: "*With* all prayer" (italics added). *With* is a connecting word. Prayer is vitally connected to Paul's discussion of spiritual warfare and the Christian's armor.

Prayer is the atmosphere in which we are to fight. It's the way we stay in vital daily contact with our Commander and activate our authority. Without prayer we don't get to use the things God has granted us. But when we access the armor of God through prayer, Satan can't touch us.

Prayer is so potent because it provides us with spiritual protection even when the battle is at its hottest. It's in prayer that we locate the ground on which we can stand firm.

It is reported that the emperor Napoleon once looked at a map and said, "If it were not for that one red dot, I could rule the world." That red dot was the British empire, the one place on the map Napoleon couldn't conquer.

Satan is a lot like Napoleon. He looks at the cross and says, "If it were not for that one red-stained cross, I could have conquered the human race."

But we escaped Satan's clutches because of that one red-stained cross. Now what we need to do is stand on what Christ has done, protected from the enemy by the power of prayer.

Prayer is necessary because it is through prayer that we engage the spiritual realm. When we pray, things happen in the heavenly places.

One of the great things about prayer is that in prayer we can hold God to His Word. There's a great example in Exodus 32:11-13, when Moses went before the Lord when God wanted to destroy the Israelites (vv. 9-10).

Moses reminded God of three things. First, these were the people He had rescued from Egypt. Second, if God destroyed the nation, the Egyptians would accuse Him of doing evil. And third, Moses reminded God of His great promises to Abraham and his descendants.

Then Exodus 32:14 says, "The Lord changed His mind." Now God was still sovereign in this situation, but from our human standpoint the intercession of Moses caused God to change His plans.

I call this putting God on the spot. Moses was able to do this in his prayer because he understood God's nature. Moses appealed to God's grace, knowing that His grace could overrule His wrath.

We have the same privilege as Moses to hold God to His Word in prayer. That fact has some tremendous implications for our spiritual warfare.

For example, if the devil has been holding you in bondage to a habit you don't believe you can break, you need to hit him with Philippians 4:13: "I can do all things through Him who strengthens me."

Do you see what I'm saying? The enemy has got us believing lies. "I can't overcome this habit." "There is no saving this marriage." "I can't be the spouse God wants me to be."

Those are bald-faced lies. If these things are really true, then God is a liar. We would never call God a liar, but that's what we do by our actions when we don't claim His Word and His power in prayer.

Prayer is also necessary because of spiritual resistance in the heavenly realm. In Daniel 10, Daniel is told that the answer to his prayer was delayed three weeks by a demon called "the prince of Persia."

Daniel's prayer was heard and answered the first day he prayed. But it took three weeks of intercessory prayer and activity on the part of the angels, especially the archangel Michael, to break the demonic blockade and get the answer through.

When we pray properly, God puts out a restraining order against the powers of darkness.

The Scope of Prayer

The scope of prayer is also included in Ephesians 6:18. We are to pray "at all times" and "with all perseverance and petition for all the saints."

The key word here is pretty obvious, isn't it? Prayer is to be made *all* the time, with *all* kinds of prayers, for *all* the saints. The scope of prayer is as wide as the world and as full as the hours in a day.

God wants us to bombard the heavenlies with our prayers. In a war, an army doesn't fire just one shell or launch one missile at the enemy. An army pounds the enemy with repeated fire.

Paul tells us to pray with perseverance. Don't "hang up" on God too soon. As Paul put it in 1 Thessalonians 5:17, "Pray without ceasing." If you're going to see this thing work, prayer cannot be an addendum to your day or week. It must be the controlling agenda of your life. We need to pray when we feel like it and when we don't.

Anybody who's serious about prayer can tell you that real prayer is hard work. Why is that? Because this is war. Satan doesn't want you to do any praying at all.

But let me give you a word of encouragement. The more intimate your relationship with God, the easier the work of prayer is. It still takes work, but it's enjoyable work when you're communing with someone you love.

Warfare Praying

I'd like to introduce you to a new way of praying. I want to help you begin to use God's Word like a sledge-hammer to break down walls and destroy fortresses. Let me tell you about what is often called warfare praying. If we are going to be soldiers, we may as well learn to pray like soldiers.

This is a new way of praying for many believers. It is praying God's Word back to Him and standing on it for victory in spiritual battle. God has such a high view of His Word that if you ever learn to pray His Word back to Him, you'll have power in prayer you never knew existed.

We need to start talking straight about our needs and using God's Word to crack the foundations of hell. Jesus dealt with Satan in the wilderness by hammering the devil with the Word. Jesus also said we must live by every word that comes from the mouth of God.

Are you praying about a problem or a situation that's so tough you wonder if it will ever be resolved? You say, "I hit it with the hammer of prayer one time, and nothing happened." Hit it again. Keep pounding on that wall with the Word of God until you see that first hairline crack. Then start praying even harder, because you know that wall is ready to come down.

Don't think I'm saying you have to do it all by your effort. Warfare praying is so powerful because our Helper is so powerful.

When Satan attacks, be faithful to do what God has

asked you to do. There is Somebody on the other side of the heavenlies to take care of the Enemy for you. "Greater is He who is in you than he who is in the world" (1 John 4:4). Keep praying, and God will make you a winner over Satan and his attacks.

YOUR ACTIONS IN SPIRITUAL WARFARE

Now that we have done all this in an attempt to understand spiritual warfare, let's take up the weapons God has given us and start assaulting the gates of hell. Let's start attacking and tearing down the strongholds that Satan has erected against us.

Let's start by defining a satanic stronghold. A stronghold is a mind-set that accepts a situation as unchangeable, even though we know that situation is contrary to the will of God.

I think it's safe to say that many people in the body of Christ are in bondage to a satanic stronghold. They have yielded ground to Satan in their lives, and he has used that ground to build an outpost from which he wages war and makes that person his prisoner of spiritual battle.

Strongholds are like fortresses. Once they get built, they are tough to attack and take out. Some of those who have Satan's strongholds in their lives have tried everything to escape, but nothing has worked.

Some strongholds are pretty obvious. Drug addiction is a satanic stronghold in which the flesh develops such a strong craving for chemicals that no matter how hard the person tries, he cannot let it go.

Some people are imprisoned by a stronghold of relationships. Another person has captured them emotionally and they are being held prisoner. For some it could even be parents who have long since died, but whose damaging influence will not allow the imprisoned person to go free.

For still other believers, the strongholds are not so obvious. They are private strongholds, fortresses of the mind and spirit that they can often hide from others. Sexual addictions such as pornography are a good example of this type of stronghold. Illicit thoughts and activities capture the mind, and people are unable to get themselves free.

Attitudes like anger, bitterness, and unforgiveness are also strongholds that we can allow Satan to construct in our hearts and minds if we are not vigilant against him.

It's unfortunate that Christians allow the devil to build his strongholds in their lives. It's even more unfortunate when they come to believe that this is the way they are doomed to live the rest of their lives because there's no way out.

Some of us blame other people for our strongholds. But people cannot cause you to surrender ground to Satan. They can certainly have an influence on you and help set you up for a stronghold. But strongholds get built when we fail to deal with sin and the devil in our own lives.

Sometimes we blame our strongholds on circumstances. A husband might say, "I wouldn't have hit my wife if she hadn't made me angry." No, all the wife did was provide an excuse for her husband's lack of control to express itself.

Someone else might say, "If they didn't have all that junk on cable television and in the movies and on the magazine racks, I wouldn't have a problem." No, all that junk does is help reveal how messed up the person with the problem really is.

Strongholds are spiritual problems, so until we attack them with our spiritual armor, they won't be torn down. The key passage here is 2 Corinthians 10:3–4, which says, "Though we walk in the flesh, we do not war according to the flesh, for the weapons of our warfare are not of the flesh, but divinely powerful for the destruction of fortresses [or strongholds]."

Remember Your Position in Christ

The first thing you must do if you want to see spiritual strongholds topple is to remember your position in Christ.

We saw above that we are already seated with Christ in the heavenly places (Ephesians 2:6). Here is the corollary action that should follow this knowledge: "If you have been raised up with Christ, keep seeking the things above, where Christ is, seated at the right hand of God. Set your mind on the things above, not on the things that are on earth" (Colossians 3:1–2).

The solution to the strongholds Satan builds in our lives is found in Christ, "for in Him all the fullness of Deity dwells in bodily form, and in Him you have been made complete, and He is the head over all rule and authority" (Colossians 2:9–10).

Christ has already beaten Satan and made a public spectacle of him (Colossians 2:15). Therefore, if you are going to beat the Evil One, you need to connect to Jesus, who won the victory over Satan.

Your exalted position in Christ also gives you legal authority over Satan so that when he attacks you, you can tell him, "You no longer have any rights or jurisdiction in my life."

I have a suspicion that there aren't many believers who understand their position in Christ well enough to announce to Satan when they are under attack, "This is an illegitimate attempt to place me under your authority. You have no rights in my life, because I have been legally set free by Christ."

That simple statement can pack a lot of power, because Satan does not want you to understand the legal authority you have in Christ. He wants you to forget who you are, because then he knows you will never exercise your legal spiritual rights.

So when the Enemy brings up your past, for instance, and tells you that you can't overcome it, you have the legal right to say, "You're a liar. I have legal papers here. Jesus has triumphed over you, and I'm with Him."

So remember—and use—your position in Christ. You are seated with Him in heaven. You have rights against Satan. He has to retreat before authority that comes from Christ.

Rely on God's Provision

Here is a second component in the process of tearing down strongholds. You must rely on God's provision.

The apostle James wrote, "[God] gives a greater grace. Therefore it says, 'God is opposed to the proud, but gives grace to the humble'" (James 4:6).

What is this "greater grace" God gives us? James is not talking about salvation, but the grace we need to live victorious lives as believers. This is the grace that is greater than the mess you may be in right now, no matter how big.

In other words, the grace God gives you to tear down strongholds is far greater than the power keeping those strongholds propped up.

If all this grace is available, the question is, How do we get it? James lined out the answer in the following verses. He began by saying, "Submit therefore to God" (James 4:7a).

Commitment doesn't work unless it is preceded by surrender.

What does that mean? Well, James gives us a great picture of what submission to God does *not* mean (vv. 1–5). You're not submitted if your life is marked by things like illicit pleasure, strife, lust, envying, and friendship with the world.

I use the term "surrender" instead of submission here because surrender is the forgotten element in submission. You don't often hear the full story when the concept of submission is taught. But if you want to submit to God so you can receive His greater grace, you need to understand all that is involved in submission.

Submission is usually presented as the process of making a commitment to Christ. That's important, but it's possible to make a commitment to the Lord without really surrendering our wills to Him.

Here's what I mean. Someone who is struggling with a stronghold can say, "I've made a commitment to the Lord, and I'm going to stop doing what I've been doing."

That sounds fine, but many people who make that kind of commitment promptly go out and fall flat on their faces. Why? Because commitment doesn't work unless it is preceded by surrender. Commitment often says, "I can," but surrender says, "Lord, I can't."

What I'm talking about is the attitude that says, "I can lick this thing myself." There's a big difference between that and realizing I need Christ's strength (Philippians 4:13). Christ's power doesn't kick in until we let go of our delusions of self-power. And that comes through surrender.

But there is still a place for commitment. Having said to God, "I can't on my own," you are now ready to say, "But through Your provision of that which I lack, I *can* go out and tear down the strongholds that are defeating me." You have now invited God to do for you what you can't do for yourself.

We are too self-sufficient, and that's why we haven't been able to tear down the strongholds. It's not that we don't try. I'm not saying that we set out to let problems and sins and failures take hold in our lives and become strongholds.

But how many times do believers promise themselves and God, "I'm going to stop doing this or that next year"? And they really mean it. They just don't have the power to carry through with their intentions. But God has something infinitely better for us than self-effort. It's called greater grace.

James continued his instruction to us: "Draw near to God and He will draw near to you" (James 4:8).

We draw near to God when we enter His presence and spend time in prayer and worship before Him. If the only worship and praise God gets out of you is on Sunday morning, you're not drawing near to Him. You're just visiting Him occasionally.

Satan is allergic to prayer. When the air is filled with prayer and praise, it chokes Satan up and makes it hard for him to function, just like pollen in the air aggravates a physical allergy. Satan can't hang around because the environment is too uncomfortable for him. Satan can't handle it when you draw near to God.

Repent of Sin

Along with remembering our position and relying

on God's provision, tearing down strongholds also involves repentance.

James wrote, "Cleanse your hands, you sinners; and purify your hearts, you double-minded. Be miserable and mourn and weep; let your laughter be turned into mourning and your joy to gloom" (4:8–9).

Admitting our sin simply means taking responsibility for it. It takes humility to admit your sin, but when you humble yourself in this way you get God's greater grace.

The opposite of humility is pride, and verse 6 goes on to say that "God is opposed to the proud." So instead of getting God's greater grace, the proud person gets God's hand in his face, resisting him and pushing him away.

Why does God push proud people away from Him? Because when we are proud we remind Him of Satan.

You can't be proud and come to God seeking His greater grace. Why? Because when you come needing grace, you don't have anything to brag about. When you need God's mercy, you can't be talking about who you are and what you have done. God wants to talk about your sin, but you want to talk about yourself. It doesn't work. Pride and humility don't mix.

Resist the Devil

I've saved this one for last even though it appears earlier in James 4: "Resist the devil and he will flee from you" (v. 7).

We have talked about dealing with the devil, but I want you to see it in the context of tearing down strongholds. The important thing is the order of these exhortations. Submitting yourself to God must come before resisting the devil.

Peter helps us here because he said the same thing. "Therefore humble yourselves under the mighty hand of God, that He may exalt you at the proper time" (1 Peter 5:6).

Why do you need to humble yourself before God? Because, Peter said, you have an enemy who walks around like "a roaring lion, seeking someone to devour" (v. 8). The devil wants to eat up your mind, chew up your circumstances, devour your joy, shred your dignity, and digest your marriage and your family.

That sounds bad, but Peter went on. You don't need to flee in fear before this lion. Instead, "resist him, firm in your faith" (v. 9). Here is the same order of events as in James. Submit to God, and you're ready to resist the devil.

One day a father and his little boy were watching the lions at the zoo when a lion let out a deafening roar. The terrified boy screamed and ran off, begging his father to run too. But his father told him to come back because the lion wouldn't hurt him.

"Son," the father said, "don't look at the lion. Look at the cage." As long as we focus on the Person and power of Christ, we won't have to worry about Satan's roar.

Put God's Word to the Test

I want to ask you a question. If we have all the authority and power we need to defeat Satan and tear down his strongholds, why don't more of us put God's Word to the test more often? What are we waiting for? Why should we pull back and cower in fear?

We have the Word of God, and we have a High Priest, Jesus Christ, whom the Bible says faced every temptation you and I will ever face (Hebrews 4:14–16). It's time to enlist in God's army and get into the battle.

Our problem today is that we have too many Christian civilians and not enough Christian soldiers. Some of us simply want to jump into a soldier's uniform when we run into a problem, rather than understanding we *are* soldiers who are supposed to be in uniform at all times because we are in a war.

You can take a major step toward victory right now by praying something like this: "Lord, I am facing Satan in these areas of my life (name the areas). I can't beat Satan on my own, so I am going to stand against him in Your name and Your strength."

When you fight the devil this week, instead of trying to prove how strong you are, tell God how weak you are. Instead of arguing you can, tell God you can't. Instead of saying, "I know I have the ability," tell God, "I don't have the ability." And then stand in the Lord's strength and His ability to deal with the Enemy in your life.

We are at war, but it's not like other wars. Christ has already won! All we have to do is enlist, put on our fatigues and our boots, and pick up our weapons, because it's time to march! It's time to win some spiritual battles.

THE URBAN ALTERNATIVE

The Philosophy

Dr. Tony Evans and TUA believe the answer to transforming our culture comes from the inside out and from the bottom up. We believe the core cause of the problems we face is a spiritual one; therefore, the only way to address them is spiritually. And that means the proclamation and application of biblical principles to the four areas of life—the individual, the family, the church, and the community. We've tried a political, social, economic, and even a religious agenda. It's time for a kingdom agenda.

The Purpose

We believe that when each biblical sphere of life functions properly, the net result is evangelism, discipleship, and community impact. As people learn how to govern themselves under God, they then transform the institutions of family, church, and government from a biblically based kingdom perspective.

The Programs

To achieve our goal we use a variety of strategies, methods, and resources for reaching and equipping as many people as possible.

- Broadcast Media
  The Urban Alternative reaches hundreds of thousands of people each day with a kingdom-based approach to life through its daily radio program, weekly television broadcast, and the Internet.

- Leadership Training
  Our national Church Development Conference, held annually, equips pastors and lay leaders to become agents of change. Teaching biblical methods of church ministry has helped congregations renew their sense of mission and expand their ministry impact.

- Crusades/Conferences
  Crusades are designed to bring churches together across racial, cultural, and denominational lines to win the lost. TUA also seeks to keep these churches together for ongoing fellowship and community impact. Conferences give Christians practical biblical insight on how to live victoriously in accordance with God's Word and His kingdom agenda in the four areas of life—personal, family, church, and community.

- Resource Development
  We are fostering lifelong learning partnerships with the people we serve by providing a variety of published materials. We offer books, audiotapes,

videos, and booklets to strengthen people in their walk with God and ministry to others.

- Project Turn-Around
  PTA is a comprehensive church-based community impact strategy. It addresses such areas as economic development, education, housing, health revitalization, family renewal and reconciliation. To model the success of the project, TUA invests in its own program locally. We also assist other churches in tailoring the model to meet the specific needs of their communities, while simultaneously addressing the spiritual and moral frame of reference.

* * *

For more information, a catalog of Dr. Tony Evans's ministry resources, and a complimentary copy of Dr. Evans's monthly devotional magazine,
call (800) 800-3222 or
write TUA at P.O. Box 4000, Dallas TX 75208.